107 Ways to Give-
When You Think You
Have Nothing to Give

Jana M. Gamble

107 Ways to Give-
When You Think You
Have Nothing to Give

Jana M. Gamble

Photograph by Saliba Photography

ISBN 978-0-9801647-3-2
Printed in the United States of America

M.O.R.E. Publishers Corp.
P.O. Box 38285
St. Louis, MO 63138
morepublishersco@aol.com

DEDICATED TO YOU!

This book is dedicated to all those who are trying to understand the calling that God has placed on your life. May God bless you and may the Holy Spirit guide you to do great things throughout this and all of your days!

CONTENTS

Inspirational Thought

If you are homeless, on welfare, unemployed, a single mother or father, disabled, uneducated, a teacher, a business owner, a lawyer, a pastor or even a multi-wealthy entrepreneur as Donald Trump - *YOU* can <u>still</u> be a giver!

Preface

The Holy Spirit led me to write *107 Ways To Give When You Think You Have Nothing To Give* as I was driving home from the St. Joachim & St. Ann Care Service. Before the revelation, I was thinking about a testimony that I had given two days prior during "Furnace Prayer" at my church, Church on The Rock. In my testimony, I explained how after 2½ months of being unemployed and receiving assistance for my rent and food for my family, I had landed a new job.

This was not just a job; it was the perfect job for me as a single mother of two. I would be able to work only Monday thru Friday. This was a blessing knowing childcare is primarily available during the same time. I also would not have to work nights, nor weekends.

I also expressed in my testimony how thankful I was for all the many blessings that I had received especially during the time of unemployment. I know for a fact that the reasons why my family never went without anything was because I put God first and acknowledged him as my source. Secondly, I am a giver.

Listening to my Pastor's teaching of the Word, reading scriptures daily, and staying inline with God's will, all enabled me to hear God's voice which prompts me daily to fulfill my calling of writing. So through this book I will share 107 ways to give.

I have personally practiced the methods myself, and some have personally blessed me. This book includes a variety of simple ways of being a giver such as sharing food from a food pantry, or being an attentive listener to someone who needs to talk. You will also read that some of my personal experiences in giving may not have always been good ones, but my goal is to go out into the world with a giving spirit!

Please remember that the most important thing is to use the resources you <u>do</u> have. Don't dwell on all that you don't have (yet)!

May this book be a blessing to both you and all the lives that you touch!

Jana M. Gamble

About the Author

JANA M. GAMBLE has been writing poetry, speeches, creating cards, etc. since childhood to inspire others and to express her own beliefs.

After placing her eyes on God and searching for her purpose in life, God spoke to her to begin her first Children's book "The Flavor of Friendship: What's Your Flavor?" in 2006 which will be available soon.

JANA M. GAMBLE is also very passionate about D. U. E. S. (Diversity, Unity, Equality, and Spirituality). She actively participates with Connections to Success/Dress for Success Midwest in both the Professional Women's Group and the Leading Ladies Leadership Series.

JANA also writes "Inspirations from an Everyday Woman" in the monthly PWG Connection Newsletter. At Church on The Rock she is involved in both the Choir and Card Ministries. Jana and her two children reside in St. Peters, Missouri.

107

Ways to Give-
When You Think You
Have Nothing to Give

"Give God your first in everything that you give or that you do."

Jana M. Gamble

107 Ways to Give....

1. Give God your first in everything that you do.
2. Give God your mind, body, and soul on a daily basis for Him to minister to and through you.
3. Replace every negative thought that enters your brain with a positive thought.

Try being positive about everything you do
for a minimum of 20 days and see how
much your life will change!

4. Make a "praise and worship" CD for someone.
5. Make a card and give it to someone for whom you've been praying.
6. Write someone a poem that will personally affect him or her.
7. Buy someone you care about something they love.

Even if your only source of income is food
stamps, you too can bless someone with
his or her favorite food!

8. Cook dinner for someone.
9. Bake and share your dessert with friends or neighbors.
10. Bless someone with food that you received. They will like the food, even if you don't care for it.

You may have got the food donated to you
from a pantry and not like it, but your
neighbors may love it. So spread the love!

7

11. Give someone a smile.

   If they smile back and have something
   in their teeth, let them know!

12. Give someone a hug.
13. When someone drops something, "for crying
    out loud", help him or her by picking it up.
14. Bless someone by leaving the quarter in
    your grocery cart at Aldi when you are
    finished. This is my favorite thing to give,
    seriously. First of all it usually takes me five
    minutes to even find a quarter. Many times
    I have to carry in pennies, dimes and nickels
    to the cashier and exchange them for a
    quarter just to get a cart so I can begin
    shopping. Plus I'm sure that it is a pleasant
    surprise for someone to go to the carts and
    find that they just got a little richer!
15. Be an attentive listener.

   Make eye contact with people!

   Don't be thinking about what
   you're getting ready to say and miss
   out on everything they're trying to
   share with you!

16. Clean someone's car for him or her.
17. Clean a friend or family member's house.
18. Let someone use your shower if they don't
    have hot water.

   You can also let someone take a
   shower just because you can
   "sense" that they need one!

19. Give someone a ride to where they need to go.
20. Give your time to someone.
21. Teach someone to draw something.
22. Help someone if they fall.

> Don't just stand there and giggle,
> help a brotha' up!

23. Help someone carry his/her groceries.
24. Push loose carts into the cart station.
25. Put personal care item samples in a special basket to leave in your bathroom for your guests.
26. Give someone correct directions.

> Yes, if you're going to give someone directions, first make sure you know where they need to go and secondly tell them if you pass ___ then you've gone too far!

27. Pick up litter off the ground.
28. Trust in God and give even if all you have left is loose change.

> Calling his disciples to him, Jesus said, *"I tell you the truth, this poor widow has put more into the treasury than all the others. They all gave out of their wealth; but she, out of her poverty, put in everything- all she had to live on."*
> The Widow's Offering - Mark 12:43-44

29. Speak to someone who looks upset. Say something uplifting to him or her.
30. Lend someone a CD of your favorite teaching.
31. Give someone a list of scriptures or quotes that will help them.
32. Invite someone new to church.
33. Invite a friend to an event.
34. Invite someone to a group meeting to which you belong.
35. Tell someone about a valuable sale.
36. Bless someone with a referral to a business/contact/website that can assist him or her.
37. Acknowledge someone.
38. Email someone something uplifting.

When you see a person you know
simply wave and say hello to them, even
if you can't remember their name.

39. Call someone that you haven't talked to for awhile.
40. Compliment someone.

Tell someone how great he or she
looks, and stop being a hater! Be
excited for the person. It is wonderful
that he or she looks amazing or is
doing something wonderful!

41. Gather a neighbor's mail when they're out of town.
42. Let someone use your computer.
43. Baby-sit for someone.

People, if you don't like watching
children don't go volunteering to
baby-sit. You'll end up sitting beside
the child and you'll both be crying for
their Momma.

44. Give someone a pen to take notes in church,
    without expecting it back. They may forget.
45. Encourage someone.
46. Share your umbrella with someone.
47. Take care of someone who is sick or hurt.
48. Give someone a massage.

How awesome is it when someone you
know is walking by you and just stops
to give you a 30- second shoulder
massage when you really needed it.
You've got to love those!

49. Donate clothes that you don't wear,
    especially the new ones.
50. Donate toys that which your children have
    stopped playing.
51. Teach something new to someone.
52. Take extra food to work and share it with
    others.

Always make sure you try the food before
you take it, for two reasons: #1 to make sure
it tastes good, and #2 because if your co-
workers are like mine all the food will be
gone before *you* even get to eat some of it.

53. Give someone a positive tip that will help
    him or her excel.

54. Hold the door open for someone.
55. Take someone's plate for him or her, after they have finished eating.
56. Let someone use your phone.
57. Get some paper towels for someone that spilled something.
58. Help redirect someone who is out of line.
59. Give someone a manicure.
60. Take a picture for someone.

There are so many opportunities to do this one. Someone will always forget the camera. Or the camera batteries will be dead, so you can offer to give them copies of your pictures, or a group of people will be looking around for someone to take their picture and you can volunteer.

61. Give your leftovers to someone who is hungry or homeless.

In 2002, I stopped at a gas station after going out to dinner with friends. I saw a homeless man rummaging through a trashcan. I felt bad for him so I quickly offered him my leftovers, I still can't believe what happened next. First he asked me "what is that?" and then said, "No, I don't want that crap." That hurt my feelings, but at least I tried to reach out to someone in need.

62. Give someone baby wipes when they or their children need them.
63. If someone is having a difficult time with multiple children or things, lend him or her a hand.
64. Call someone that missed church and share your notes.
65. Participate in a porch pickup donation process such as the ones Vietnam Veterans of America have, or what the Scouts do.
66. Lend a friend some movies that they haven't seen, and/or inform them where to get free videos.

Both of those were great benefits to
my family especially during the time
that we didn't have cable.

67. Give someone a new recipe.
68. Invite a friend to exercise with you.
69. Lend a friend a book or magazine that will be beneficial to them.
70. Make a special day that's not a holiday to celebrate your love for someone.
71. Participate in www.freecycle.com or a similar process.

You can receive great blessings and
be amazed in seeing what people are
"just giving away for free!"

72. Plant flowers, fruits, or vegetables and share your harvest.

73. Either through money, donations, or prayers. Give back to where you came from.

The many journeys we travel in life
may seem to be very minute to us or
tremendous instead, but no matter
where you have arrived in life give
thanks to those who supported you
along the way. Even still, give thanks
to those who told you that you
wouldn't make it, because they were
the fuel that made your inner drive
strive just a little harder!

74. Give up negative habits.

If you give up one negative habit,
what sense does it make to replace
it with another negative habit?

75. Be supportive and attend something special
for a friend.

Sometimes you need to stop and think
about what is important to a friend. Yes,
they may have invited 30 other people to
come but knowing that you will be there
gives him or her so much more
confidence in their heart.

76. Donate your hair to Locks of Love or a
similar program.
77. Be nice to someone even if you feel they
don't deserve it.
78. Forgive yourself or someone else that has
hurt you.

You can't heal emotionally until you have
forgiven whoever has hurt you. Who are
we to NOT forgive another soul on this
earth when God forgives each person
under his beautiful blue sky four-hundred
and ninety times every single day!

79. Serve in your calling as the Holy Spirit
    leads you.
80. Give God your spirit so that you can hear
    directions from the Holy Spirit.

It's natural to want to try new things on
your own. Have you experienced the
supernatural first time? When you know
your calling it is highly important to
follow the promptings from the Holy
Spirit. Look at the difference between the
events where you obeyed a prompting and
those when you didn't. You're guaranteed
to be in line with your vision and God's
will when you listen, not to mention you
will save yourself a lot of time and money.

81. Give a word of hope to someone who is
    hopeless.
82. Give an apology to someone to whom you
    owe one.
83. Give God your obedience.

Obey (obedience) means to do as asked, to
yield to someone's commands or wishes.
(Also see Luke 17:7-10)

84. Give God your praise.

85. Be patient with something or someone that is being difficult.
86. Give yourself a scripture to be quoted every time you start to get frustrated.

"Greater is He that is in me..."

87. Feed your spirit daily. (The Bible is spirit food).
88. Give someone a piece of gum or a mint.
89. Give someone a tissue when they're crying.

It's embarrassing enough to be crying in front of people. Give the person a tissue before they have to start wiping tears and a runny nose with their hands.

90. Carry Tylenol with you so you can share it with someone who needs it.
91. Mow someone's lawn.
92. Take out someone's trash for him or her.
93. Rake someone's leaves.
94. Shovel someone's driveway and sidewalk.
95. Help cleanup when you are not assigned to do so.

More often than not, when you attend an event and it has come to an end, the same people who set it all up are the very ones who are assigned to clean up the mess you and your friends just made over the last several hours. I guarantee that if you at least help by clearing away your own mess or even more, someone will be extremely thankful that you lent a hand.

96. Give a coat or blanket to some that is cold.
97. Use the gifts God gave you to bless others.
98. Give someone a band-aid when they get hurt.
99. Warm someone's car up for them.

Why not take turns with fellow
employees that you trust and let one
person go out in the cold and warm up
a couple of cars. You will all be able
leave in warmer cars.

100. Scrape the ice off someone's car windows.
101. Help someone jump-start their car or use your jumper cables.
102. Help someone repair his or her car.

Now if you don't know how to fix cars,
please do not sit there and help make the
person's problem even worse. Hey, be
honest and say, "I have no idea what to
do, but I can hold the flashlight and hand
the tools to you if that'll help!"

103. Share coupons with friends that can use them.
104. Give someone a makeover.
105. Bless someone with a haircut.
106. Bless someone with a gas card.
107. Let someone in front of you, while you are waiting in a line or in traffic.

Look, you're already waiting in a long line anyhow, right? Okay, so instead of "acting" as if you are ignoring the person staring at you and speeding up real quickly to not allow them to join you in the waiting game, give them a little wave and let them get in front of you.

The Giving Guide

It's amazing how God perfectly orchestrates His works. When we give something, God will always reward us by blessing us back with it and usually in an even greater way. Be a giver because we were placed on this Earth to help others- not solely for the intention of gaining something for self.

Also, always remember to be cautious that you are not being an enabler, but that you are actually helping those to whom you are giving. As in anything you may choose to do, pray and seek guidance from the Holy Spirit so that you may be a vessel that God can use to fill a need.

Personally, giving makes me feel wonderful inside. Honestly if I'm not feeling great, then I always find a way to brighten up someone else's day. Seeing them smile makes me feel better as well.

These "107 Ways to Give..." are very basic and just the beginning to all that you can potentially give! Now that you have read all the 107 Ways, use the rest of this book to help you grow in *your* giving.

Giving Goals

If you are ambitious about developing into a giver without *any* action, then you will <u>not</u> get anything accomplished. In order to become a great giver you should start by writing down some specific goals. These goals will serve as a reminder for you and can help you to monitor your progress.

My Great Giving Goals

Date Goals Were Set: _____

• Daily I will

_____

_____

• Weekly I will

_____

_____

• Once a month I will

_____

_____

• One time this year I will

_____

_____

• My Ultimate giving goal is to

_____

_____

_____

_____

My Giving List (Weekly)

Date	What I did	My results
(example) 01/04/08	I gave my time to help my friend who was injured.	It enabled him to relax and not worry because I was there to help

Date	What I did	My results

Date	What I did	My results

Date	What I did	My results

Date	What I did	My results

Date	What I did	My results

Date	What I did	My results

Date	What I did	My results

Date	What I did	My results

Date	What I did	My results

Date	What I did	My results

Date	What I did	My results

Date	What I did	My results

Date	What I did	My results

Date	What I did	My results

Date	What I did	My results

My Giving Journal

When I give I feel:

_____

_____

_____

_____

_____

_____

_____

_____

My favorite act of giving is:

_____

_____

_____

_____

_____

_____

_____

_____

_____

_____

When someone gives to me I feel:

_____

_____

_____

_____

_____

_____

_____

_____

_____

"I am a Giver!"

_____

_____

_____

_____

_____

_____

_____

_____

_____

_____

_____

_____

_____

_____

"I am a Giver!"

_____

_____

_____

_____

_____

_____

_____

_____

_____

_____

_____

_____

_____

_____

"I am a Giver!"

_____

_____

_____

_____

_____

_____

_____

_____

_____

_____

_____

_____

_____

_____

"I am a Giver!"

_____

_____

_____

_____

_____

_____

_____

_____

_____

_____

_____

_____

_____

_____

"I am a Giver!"

"I am a Giver!"

_____

_____

_____

_____

_____

_____

_____

_____

_____

_____

_____

_____

_____

"I am a Giver!"

_____

_____

_____

_____

_____

_____

_____

_____

_____

_____

_____

_____

_____

_____

"I am a Giver!"

_____

_____

_____

_____

_____

_____

_____

_____

_____

_____

_____

_____

_____

_____

_____

"I am a Giver!"

_____

_____

_____

_____

_____

_____

_____

_____

_____

_____

_____

_____

_____

_____

"I am a Giver!"

"I am a Giver!"

_____

_____

_____

_____

_____

_____

_____

_____

_____

_____

_____

_____

_____

_____

"I am a Giver!"

_____

_____

_____

_____

_____

_____

_____

_____

_____

_____

_____

_____

_____

_____

_____

"I am a Giver!"

_____

_____

_____

_____

_____

_____

_____

_____

_____

_____

_____

_____

_____

_____

"I am a Giver!"

_____

_____

_____

_____

_____

_____

_____

_____

_____

_____

_____

_____

_____

_____

"I am a Giver!"

_____

_____

_____

_____

_____

_____

_____

_____

_____

_____

_____

_____

_____

"I am a Giver!"

_____

_____

_____

_____

_____

_____

_____

_____

_____

_____

_____

_____

_____

_____

The Giver's Prayer

I am a giver
A God-like example others can see

I am a giver
No matter how big or small my gift may be

I am a giver
Never acting for what I could possibly gain

I am a giver
Even when I go through trials and pain

I am a giver
Because it's the least I can do

I am a giver
Because Jesus gave His life for me and for
YOU!

By *Jana M. Gamble*

A Final Thought

Always remember that God gave
YOU
something to offer this world that only
YOU
can give because
YOU
are *uniquely* made in His image!

Readers' Comments

"Motivating and inspiring! A great book to have on hand to remind you how to make a difference."
Haley Abell

"Reading this book makes you want to be a better person. It inspires me to look outside of myself and make a difference in the world."
Jo Stahl

"A very spiritual perspective on ways to help and maintain a positive attitude throughout life's ups and downs!"
Sandra Price

"I was honored that you asked me to review your book. I have enjoyed reading it. You make some profound statements in your book that makes one think. A lot of people will benefit from your creative writing ability."
Lisa Bell, author

95139986R00039